TALYLLYN
50 years of change

Vic Mitchell

MP Middleton Press

*Cover pictures: Upper - **Dolgoch** waits at Towyn Wharf on 11th August 1950, with the entire fleet of coaches standing at various angles. (D.Trevor Rowe) Lower - In contrast, excellent track is seen at the other terminus of the line on 28th August 1998, as **Sir Haydn** runs round its train of immaculate coaches. (V.Mitchell)*

First published January 2000

ISBN 1 901706 39 7

Design David Pede

Published by
Middleton Press
Easebourne Lane
Midhurst, West Sussex
GU29 9AZ
Tel: 01730 813169
Fax: 01730 812601

Printed & bound by Biddles Ltd,
Guildford and Kings Lynn

INDEX

AUTHOR'S NOTES

Having admired the Kerr Stuart 0-4-2Ts of the narrow gauge Hampton Waterworks system as a small child, I had to satisfy myself with the footplate of a T9 shunting the local goods yard for most of my schooldays. In my final school term I read of the takeover, by enthusiasts, of the Talyllyn Railway.

At the earliest opportunity I set off for Wales with a good friend, a small tent and high hopes of an intimate encounter with the narrow gauge, so greatly missed. We arrived 16 days after the resumption of regular services and were put to work replacing the keys above Dolgoch.

We were conveyed from Wharf to Pendre on the running plate of *Dolgoch* - it was then that we realised why it had an unusual brass rail along the top of its boiler. (Hapless firemen also held onto it to practise unilateral sanding). To our alarm we watched the far ends of some rails rise out of the turf and then descend again, as the engine proceeded with a rhythmic thump at each loose joint. The crew could not see it so clearly!

Alan French and I spent several happy days in the company of the now well known preservation pioneers, an educational experience unparalleled previously in our lives and to remain everlasting in our memories. How grateful we are to them for their enterprise and foresight.

We joined the sole member of the permanent way staff and began digging out fragments of rotten timber that once represented sleepers, prior to the insertion of new ones near Towyn. At the end of the week, we were taken by road to Dolgoch, where we were sent on our way for a weekend of emergency work east thereof. This is described in captions 83 and 84.

I am also pleased to have had the friendship of Allan Garraway since those days and to have published *Garraway Father & Son*, particularly since it contains a chapter detailing the TR revival, as well as mention of the day on which he pushed his penknife right through the firebox wall of the line's only operational locomotive!

The successes and frustrations of the pioneers in the early 1950s are vividly described by L.T.C.Rolt in his classic *Railway Adventure*. It is recommended to all interested in the line, despite recent reprints having a photo of your author and friend, unnamed and unwashed, working on the track with Rolt.

The compilation of this album has been aided greatly by David Mitchell, who is no relation but is chairman of the Talyllyn Railway Preservation Society. He has had a long association with the line, photographed it extensively and provided access to the TRPS collection of pictures. To all these contributors, I express my great gratitude.

I am also grateful for the help received from John Bate, for he has been actively involved with the TR for almost 50 years, latterly as its civil and mechanical engineer; he has amended many of the facts that have been incorrectly published previously, as has John Slater. As usual David and Susan Salter have been most helpful and Godfrey Croughton has provided tickets copies.

My sincere appreciation also goes to my dear wife, Barbara, who has typeset this and 136 other albums. We met in 1952 and she has subsequently supported all my railway (and other) escapades enthusiastically. God bless her.

Vic Mitchell Midhurst, September 1999

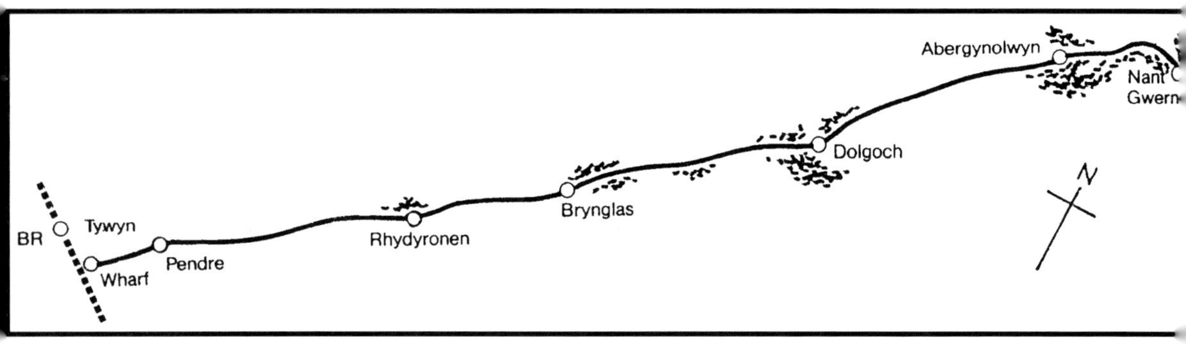

The route map shows the line as used by passenger trains since 1976. The dotted areas represent woodland. (Railway Magazine)

GEOGRAPHICAL SETTING

The railway was named after a lake, which was more than three miles from its eastern terminus at Abergynolwyn. This village is situated at the confluence of the Afon Dysynni, which drains Tal-y-Llyn Lake, and the Nant Gwernol which rises to the south, near the Bryn Eglwys Quarries, now disused. The river flows to the north and then west to reach the sea through a valley parallel to the one in which the railway was constructed.

Thus there is little in the way of a watercourse to be seen in the valley on a downward journey until reaching Dolgoch, where the Afon Fathew falls spectacularly and passes under the line.

The valley widens greatly for the final two miles of the journey to Tywyn (spelt Towyn until 1975 and used aptly in this volume), which is situated on the coastal plain, nearly one mile from Cardigan Bay. The town had a population of around 2000 at the time of the railway's revival.

The cutting between Wharf and Pendre was deepened in 1978-79 to give a more uniform gradient of about 1 in 120. The profile above Abergynolwyn was made less erratic in the early 1970s.

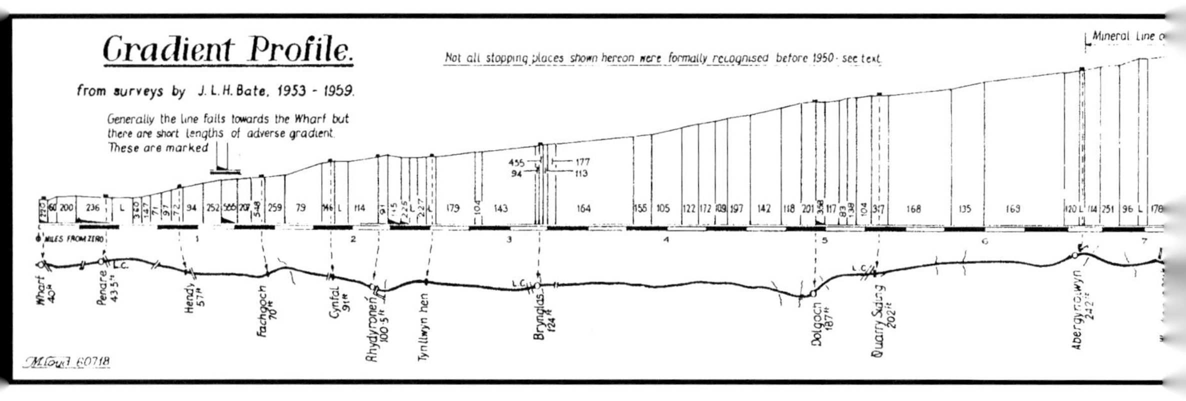

HISTORICAL BACKGROUND

Slate quarries were developed at Bryn Eglwys in the mid-1860s and an Act of Parliament was obtained on 5th July 1865 to construct a 2ft 3ins gauge railway to the coast. It was also to convey passengers between Abergynolwyn and a station near the town of Towyn (at Pendre), a distance of a little over six miles. This traffic began in December 1866, the railway and the quarries having common ownership. Mineral traffic had commenced before the Act was passed.

There was an extension at Towyn for slate and goods traffic to a wharf alongside the standard gauge railway, which had opened from Aberdovey on 24th October 1863. It was extended northwards in August 1867.

The quarries, and thus the railway, had a mixed fortune and were purchased in 1911 by the local MP, Mr Haydn Jones.

Since its construction, very little changed on the railway. Quarrying ceased in 1946 but the owner (by then knighted) continued to run trains, albeit at a loss. His death at the age of 86 in July 1950 would have resulted in closure and scrapping had not a group of enthusiasts, led by author L.T.C.Rolt, thought otherwise.

During the following October, meetings were held which resulted in the formation of the Tal-y-Llyn Railway Preservation Society and Sir Haydn's executors allowed the railway to be operated by amateurs in 1951. His widow graciously donated the line to the new organisation and its future was thus more assured.

Significantly, the first train of the preservation era ran to Rhydyronen on Whit Monday 1951, a world first. A Monday to Friday service commenced on 4th June of that year, this leaving the weekends free for work on the decrepit and unreliable equipment. A film scriptwriter visited the line that Summer and was inspired to create the "Titfield Thunderbolt". Sadly it was not filmed on the TR (see *Frome to Bristol* for the location), but it raised awareness of the scheme. It was to be 1954 before the line could be considered secure.

The inclusion of "Preservation" in the Society's title proved inappropriate in view of the neglected and rickety condition of the line. Changes were necessary on grounds of safety and to meet the needs of tourists, whose pockets and purses ensured the railway's survival.

To increase line capacity, passing loops were required; these are detailed in the captions. Extension of passenger operation to Nant Gwernol took place on 22nd May 1976, this giving visitors an added scenic pleasure.

Many of the necessary and unavoidable changes are illustrated in this volume and much of the work of the large number of volunteers and the small permanent staff is recorded with appreciation of their efforts.

PASSENGER SERVICES

In the final Summers of Sir Haydn Jones' ownership, a morning and an afternoon return trip was advertised for Mondays, Wednesdays and Fridays, but they were not always operated, due to the failure of the one remaining operable locomotive.

The new management announced a similar timetable but to run five days per week and each journey to take 15 minutes longer, to conserve the ailing rolling stock and track. Thus, few trains were cancelled. The same service was offered in the Summer of 1952, but with the addition of a Saturday afternoon train. For 1952 and 1953, an evening train was added for the five peak weeks.

A Fridays-only shoppers service was provided in the Winter of 1952-53, between Pendre and Brynglas. In the Summers of 1957-58, there were departures from Town Wharf at 10.25am, 2.10pm (stopping at Dolgoch only) and 3.0pm on Mondays to Fridays, only the latter train running on Saturdays. A Sunday train was introduced in 1959, leaving at 2.50pm in the peak Summer weeks.

Subsequent decades have seen steadily increasing frequencies, geared carefully to the tourist season. The loops (described in the captions) have permitted improvements. Passing of two trains became common practice in 1953, three in 1969 and four in 1976.

Tal-y-llyn Railway

(The oldest surviving passenger carrying narrow gauge railway in the world).

No visit to Wales is complete without a journey on this historic railway which traverses seven miles of magnificent mountain scenery from the sea coast to Dolgoch Falls and Abergynolwyn near the slopes of Cader Idris.

TIME TABLE

JUNE 4th. to SEPTEMBER 28th. 1951.

Up Trains (Mondays to Fridays inclusive).

		a.m.	p.m.
ABERDOVEY (B.R.)	*Dep.*	*8.41*	*1.20*
BARMOUTH JUNC. (B.R.)	,,	*9.35*	*2.0*
TOWYN (Wharf)	,,	10.30	2.45
TOWYN (Pendre)	,,	10.35	2.50
RHYDYRONEN	,,	10.45	3.0
BRYNGLAS	,,	10.55	3.10
DOLGOCH	,,	11.10	3.25
ABERGYNOLWYN	*Arr.*	11.30	3.45

Down Trains (Mondays to Fridays inclusive).

		a.m.	p.m.
ABERGYNOLWYN	*Dep.*	11.45	4.0
DOLGOCH	,,	12.5	4.20
BRYNGLAS	,,	12.20	4.35
RHYDYRONEN	,,	12.30	4.45
TOWYN (Pendre)	,,	12.40	4.55
TOWYN (Wharf)	*Arr.*	12.45	5.0
BARMOUTH JUNC. (B.R.)	,,	*1.40*	*6.38*
ABERDOVEY (B.R.)	,,	*1.6*	*6.17*

Towyn Wharf terminus is 3 minutes walk from Towyn B.R. station. Special trains may be run for organised parties on Saturdays only by prior arrangement.

L. T. C. ROLT,
General Manager,

TOWYN and ABERGYNOLWYN.—Tal-y-llyn.

Runs 25th May to 26th September inclusive.

Miles	Up	Week Days a.m (Except Saturdays)	p.m		p.m (Runs 27th July to 22nd August)
	Towyn (Wharf) ...dep	10 25	2 55	..	6 20
	" (Pendre)	10 30	3 0	..	6 25
2½	Rhydyronen	10 42	3 12	..	6 37
3¼	Brynglas	10 48	3 18	..	6 43
5	Dolgoch for The Falls	11 5	3 35	..	7 0
7	Abergynolwyn K .arr	11 20	3 50	..	7 15

Miles	Down	Week Days a.m (Except Saturdays)	p.m		p.m (Runs 27th July to 22nd August)
	Abergynolwyn...dep	1145	4 50	..	7 35
2	Dolgoch for The Falls	12 0	5 5	..	7 50
3¼	Brynglas	1217	5 22	..	8 7
4¼	Rhydyronen	1223	5 28	..	8 13
6¼	Towyn (Pendre)	1235	5 40	..	8 25
7	" (Wharf) ...arr	1240	5 45	..	8 30

K Station for Nant Gwernol.
Trains also call by request at the following Halts, Hen-dy, Fach Goch, Cynfal and Tyn-y-Llwyn
Subject to alteration from 30th June to 9th July inclusive.

Bradshaw 1953

Bradshaw 1956

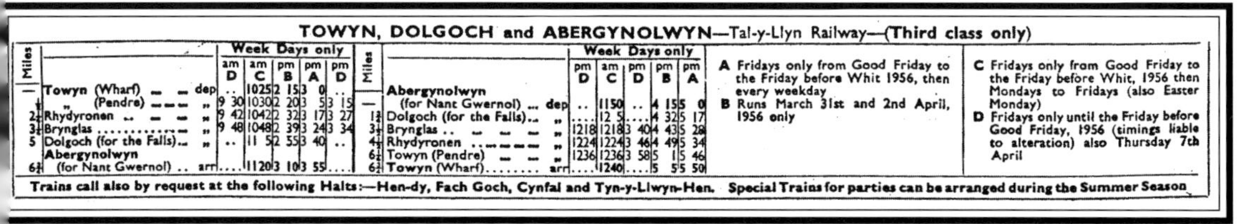

TOWYN, DOLGOCH and ABERGYNOLWYN—Tal-y-Llyn Railway—(Third class only)

Miles		Week Days only am D	am C	pm B	pm A	pm D
—	Towyn (Wharf) ... dep	..	1025	2 15	3 0	..
	" (Pendre) ... "	9 30	1030	2 20	3 5	3 15
2½	Rhydyronen ... "	9 42	1042	2 32	3 17	3 27
3¼	Brynglas ... "	9 48	1048	2 39	3 24	3 34
5	Dolgoch (for the Falls) ... "	..	11 5	2 55	3 40	..
6¾	Abergynolwyn (for Nant Gwernol) .. arr	....	1120	3 10	3 55	..

Miles		Week Days only pm D	am C	pm D	pm B	pm A
—	Abergynolwyn (for Nant Gwernol) ... dep	..	1150	..	4 15	5 0
1½	Dolgoch (for the Falls) ... "	....	12 5	..	4 32	5 17
3¼	Brynglas ... "	1218	1218	3 40	4 43	5 28
4¼	Rhydyronen ... "	1224	1224	3 46	4 49	5 34
6	Towyn (Pendre) ... "	1236	1236	3 58	5 1	5 46
6¾	Towyn (Wharf) ... arr	....	1240	..	5 5	5 50

A Fridays only from Good Friday to the Friday before Whit 1956, then every weekday
B Runs March 31st and 2nd April, 1956 only
C Fridays only from Good Friday to the Friday before Whit, 1956 then Mondays to Fridays (also Easter Monday)
D Fridays only until the Friday before Good Friday, 1956 (timings liable to alteration) also Thursday 7th April

Trains call also by request at the following Halts:—Hen-dy, Fach Goch, Cynfal and Tyn-y-Llwyn-Hen. Special Trains for parties can be arranged during the Summer Season

TOWYN, DOLGOCH and ABERGYNOLWYN—Tal-y-Llyn Railway—(One class only)

	Week Days am E		pm A	pm B	pm	pm A	Suns pm F
Towyn (Wharf) ... dep	1025	..	1 15	2 0	3 0	3 50	3 0
" (Pendre) ... "	1030	..	..	..	3 5	dd	dd
Rhydyronen ... "	1040	..	..	..	3 15	dd	dd
Brynglas ... "	1046	..	..	..	3 20	dd	dd
Dolgoch (for the Falls) "	11 0	..	1 45	2 35	3 35	4 30	3 30
Abergynolwyn (for Nant Gwernol) arr	1110	..	1 55	2 45	3 45	4 40	3 40

	Week Days am E	pm A	pm A	pm B	pm	Suns pm F
Abergynolwyn (for Nant Gwernol) dep	1150	2 0	2 55	4 45	5 0	4 30
Dolgoch (for the Falls) "	12 3	2 8	3 5	5 0	5 15	4 45
Brynglas ... "	1213	..	..	..	5 25	dd
Rhydyronen ... "	1219	..	..	..	5 31	dd
Towyn (Pendre) "	1229	..	..	..	5 41	dd
Towyn (Wharf) ... arr	1234	2 45	3 40	5 30	5 45	5 10

A Except Saturdays and runs 25th July to 26th August
B Runs 18th July to 2nd September
dd Calls if required
E Except Saturdays
F Not after 4th September

Special Trains for parties can be arranged during the Summer Season

Trains call also by request at the following Halts:—Hen-dy, Fach Goch, Cynfal, Tyn-y-Llwyn-Hen and Quarry Siding.

radshaw from June 1960

R 1975

Miles			Tuesdays, Wednesdays, Thursdays and Sundays 7 to 16 May and 29 Sept. to 27 October			Mondays to Fridays 20 to 24 May, 3 to 14 June, 2 to 27 September A		B		Saturdays 18 May 1, 8, 15 June, 7, 14, 21 Sep.			Sundays 19 May 2, 9, 16 June, 8, 15 22 Sep.		
0	Towyn Wharf	d	..	14 30	..	10 15	12 30	13 50	14 50	..	14 30	..	12 30	14 50	..
¾	Towyn Pendre †	d	..	14 35	..	10 20	12 35		14 55	..	14 35	..	12 35	14 55	..
2½	Rhydyronen †	d	..	14 44	..	10 29	12 44		15 04	..	14 44	..	12 44	15 04	..
3¼	Brynglas †	d	..	14 50	..	10 35	12 50		15 10	..	14 50	..	12 50	15 10	..
5	Dolgoch Falls	d	..	15 00	..	10 45	13 00	14 20	15 20	..	15 00	..	13 00	15 20	..
6¾	Abergynolwyn	a	..	15 15	..	11 00	13 15	14 30	15 35	..	15 15	..	13 15	15 35	..

Miles			Tuesdays, Wednesdays, Thursdays and Sundays 7 to 16 May and 29 Sept. to 27 October			Mondays to Fridays 20 to 24 May, 3 to 14 June, 2 to 27 September A		B		Saturdays 18 May 1, 8, 15 June, 7, 14, 21 Sep.			Sundays 19 May 2, 9, 16 June, 8, 15 22 Sep.		
0	Abergynolwyn	d	..	15 45	..	11 25	13 45	14 45	15 50	..	15 50	..	13 45	15 50	..
1½	Dolgoch Falls	d	..	16 00	..	11 40	14 00	15 00	16 05	..	16 05	..	14 00	16 05	..
3¼	Brynglas †	d	..	16 09	..	11 49	14 09	15 09	16 14	..	16 14	..	14 09	16 14	..
4¼	Rhydyronen †	d	..	16 15	..	11 55	14 15	15 15	16 20	..	16 20	..	14 15	16 20	..
6	Towyn Pendre †	d	..	16 24	..	12 04	14 24	15 24	16 29	..	16 29	..	14 24	16 29	..
6¾	Towyn Wharf	a	..	16 28	..	12 08	14 28	15 28	16 33	..	16 33	..	14 28	16 33	..

25 May to 31 May and 17 June to 12 July

	Mondays to Fridays	FX					Saturdays and Sundays				
Towyn Wharf d	10 15	11 15	12 15		16 15	..	..	12 30	..	14 50	..
Towyn Pendre † d	10 20	11 20	12 20	and	16 20	..	..	12 35	..	14 55	..
Rhydyronen † d	10 29	11 29	12 29	every	16 29	..	..	12 44	..	15 04	..
Brynglas † d	10 35	11 35	12 35	hour	16 35	..	..	12 50	..	15 10	..
Dolgoch Falls d	10 45	11 45	12 45	until	16 45	..	..	13 00	..	15 20	..
Abergynolwyn a	11 00	12 00	13 00		17 00	..	..	13 15	..	15 35	..

	Mondays to Fridays	FX					Saturdays and Sundays				
Abergynolwyn d	11 10	12 10	13 10		17 10	..	..	13 45	..	15 50	..
Dolgoch Falls d	11 25	12 25	13 25	and	17 25	..	..	14 00	..	16 05	..
Brynglas † d	11 34	12 34	13 34	every	17 34	..	..	14 09	..	16 14	..
Rhydyronen † d	11 41	12 41	13 41	hour	17 41	..	..	14 15	..	16 20	..
Towyn Pendre † d	11 50	12 50	13 50	until	17 50	..	..	14 24	..	16 29	..
Towyn Wharf a	11 55	12 55	13 55		17 55	..	..	14 28	..	16 33	..

13 July to 1 September

Mondays to Fridays

											FX	C WO	
Towyn Wharf .. d	10 15	10 45	11 15	12 15	12 45	13 15	14 15	14 45	15 15	16 15	16 45	19 20	..
Towyn Pendre † d	10 20	10 50	11 20	12 20	12 50	13 20	14 20	14 50	15 20	16 20	16 50	19 25	..
Rhydyronen † d	10 29	10 59	11 29	12 29	12 59	13 29	14 29	14 59	15 29	16 29	16 59	19 34	..
Brynglas † d	10 35	11 05	11 37	12 37	13 07	13 37	14 37	15 07	15 37	16 37	17 07	19 40	..
Dolgoch Falls d	10 45	11 15	11 49	12 49	13 19	13 49	14 49	15 19	15 49	16 49	17 19	19 50	..
Abergynolwyn a	11 00	11 30	12 00	13 00	13 30	14 00	15 00	15 30	16 00	17 00	17 30	20 05	..

											FX	C WO	
Abergynolwyn d	11 15	11 45	12 15	13 15	13 45	14 15	15 15	15 45	16 15	17 15	17 45	20 30	..
Dolgoch Falls d	11 25	11 55	12 25	13 25	13 55	14 25	15 25	15 55	16 25	17 25	17 55	20 45	..
Brynglas † d	11 35	12 05	12 35	13 35	14 05	14 35	15 35	16 05	16 35	17 35	18 05	20 54	..
Rhydyronen † d	11 42	12 12	12 42	13 42	14 12	14 42	15 42	16 12	16 42	17 42	18 12	21 00	..
Towyn Pendre † d	11 49	12 19	12 49	13 49	14 19	14 49	15 49	16 19	16 49	17 49	18 19	21 09	..
Towyn Wharf a	11 55	12 25	12 55	13 55	14 25	14 55	15 55	16 25	16 55	17 55	18 25	21 13	..

Saturdays / Sundays

	Saturdays					D	Sundays					E
Towyn Wharf .. d	..	12 45	13 45	14 45	15 45	19 20	10 30	12 45	13 45	14 45	15 45	19 20
Towyn Pendre † d	..	12 50	13 50	14 50	15 50	19 25	10 35	12 50	13 50	14 50	15 50	19 25
Rhydyronen † d	..	12 59	13 59	14 59	15 59	19 34	10 44	12 59	13 59	14 59	15 59	19 34
Brynglas † d	..	13 05	14 05	15 05	16 05	19 40	10 50	13 05	14 05	15 05	16 05	19 40
Dolgoch Falls d	..	13 18	14 18	15 18	16 18	19 50	11 00	13 18	14 18	15 18	16 18	19 50
Abergynolwyn a	..	13 30	14 30	15 30	16 30	20 05	11 15	13 30	14 30	15 30	16 30	20 05

	Saturdays					D	Sundays					E
Abergynolwyn d	..	13 45	14 45	15 45	16 45	20 30	11 35	13 45	14 45	15 45	16 45	20 30
Dolgoch Falls d	..	13 55	14 51	15 55	16 55	20 45	11 50	13 55	14 55	15 55	16 55	20 45
Brynglas † d	..	14 05	15 05	16 05	17 05	20 54	11 59	14 05	15 05	16 05	17 05	20 54
Rhydyronen † d	..	14 12	15 12	16 12	17 12	21 00	12 05	14 12	15 12	16 12	17 12	21 00
Towyn Pendre † d	..	14 19	15 19	16 19	17 19	21 09	12 14	14 19	15 19	16 19	17 19	21 09
Towyn Wharf a	..	14 25	15 25	16 25	17 25	21 13	12 18	14 25	15 25	16 25	17 25	21 13

† Trains call at these stations as required at the times shown: also as required at Hendy, Fach Goch, Cynfal, Tynyllwyn-hen and Quarry Siding. Passengers wishing to alight must give notice at the time of booking. Passengers desirin to join must give an appropriate hand signal to the driver

A Until 20 September
B 2 to 6 September
C 17 July to 21 August
D Until 24 August
E Until 25 August

TOWYN WHARF

1. No. 2 *Dolgoch* stands with the railway's complete passenger stock in July 1951. The leading coach was built by the Lancaster Wagon Co. and the following three, together with the guards van, came from Brown, Marshalls & Co. All this equipment was over 80 years old, as was the other locomotive, no. 1 *Talyllyn*, by then inoperable. Both had been built by Fletcher, Jennings in Whitehaven. (A.G.W.Garraway)

→

2. Another 1951 view of *Dolgoch* includes the Wharf offices in which there was no provision for passengers, other than the issuing of tickets. There was one wooden bench outside but no platform. The solitary gas light was on the public highway. (Ll.Bedder)

→

3. During the Winter of 1951-52, a platform was built, the track was relaid with visible sleepers and a loop provided. Prior to 1951, empty trains were propelled to Pendre, where the locomotive ran round its train, the coaches usually being returned by gravity. During 1951, the train was reversed out of the station, the coaches were braked and uncoupled, *Dolgoch* ran forward into a siding and then the train returned under gravity. The line's first internal combustion locomotive is being unloaded in September 1952; it was numbered 5 but it was unsuccessful and did not remain for long. The power unit had come from Rolt's canal boat; it had been made for a Model T Ford. (Ll.Bedder)

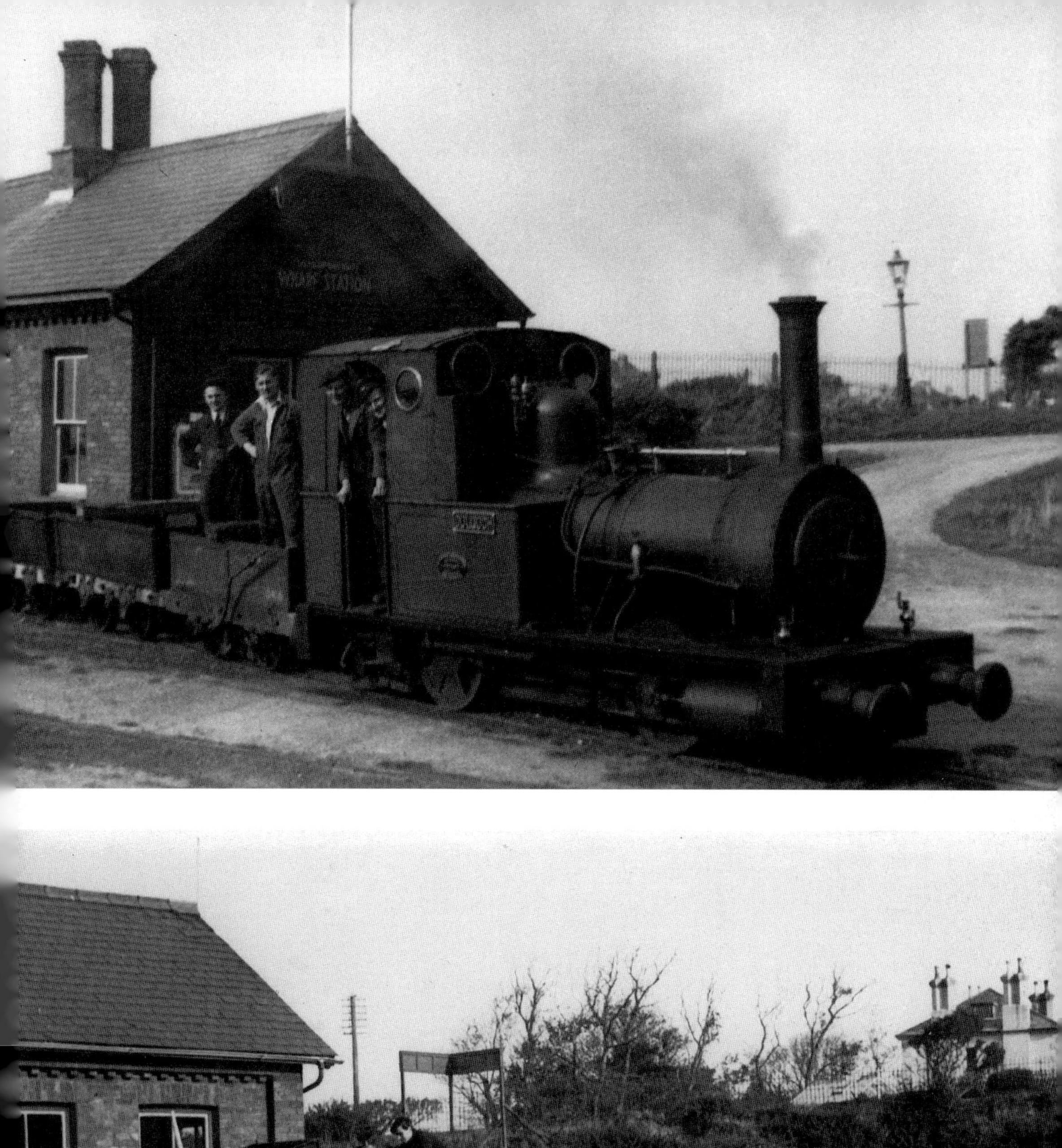

EDWARD THOMAS

ERF

←

4. No. 4 *Edward Thomas* was one of two former Corris Railway locomotives bought by the TR in 1951. It had been built by Kerr Stuart in 1921 and was repaired by Hunslet in 1951-52 to become regarded as the line's saviour at that time. It was photographed at the end of the line in 1953, with the former slate loaders cabin in the background. (J.J.Davis)

6. Seen prior to the TRPS AGM on 26th September 1953 are (from left to right) nos. 2, 3 and 4. No. 3 was also from the Corris Railway but was built by Hughes in Loughborough in 1878 and was given the name *Sir Haydn* on the TR. Their purchase price in March 1951 was £25 each. (J.J.Davis)

←

5. The slate loading wharf in the foreground was used for unloading locomotive coal until BR withdrew freight service on the coast line in 1984. No.6 *Douglas* is about to be unloaded on 19th July 1954. No.2 *Dolgoch* is to the left of it and will soon be propelled onto the trailer, prior to a major overhaul in the Midlands. No.4 is on the right. (J.C.Flemon/TR coll.)

WHARF STATION

←

7. A photograph of the bridge rebuilding in March 1955 includes the weighbridge outside the office and the former gunpowder store (right). All the necessities of life had once been loaded here for conveyance to Abergynolwyn. (R.K.Walton)

←

8. Another platform face was constructed during 1955, as can be seen in this September view, but it was never used. The morning train is headed by no. 6 *Douglas*, which had been built by Andrew Barclay in 1918 and arrived on the TR in 1954, to become its fifth steam locomotive. (J.J.Davis)

9. For the AGM delegates in 1955, the TRPS hired a special train from Paddington, the locomotives on the final leg of the journey being ex-LSWR class T9 no. 30304 and ex-GWR 4-4-0 no. 9027. Other members wait on the little used wharf. The first such special had been in 1953, when a single ex-GWR railcar, devoid of toilet, ran from London. The return took 13½ hours. (J.J.Davis)

10. It was deemed appropriate to establish a museum of narrow gauge equipment on the site. One notable item of interest that arrived for storage was the two-foot gauge 2-6-2T *Russell*. It has had a complex history and no longer stands near the gunpowder store, where it was photographed in 1955, but has returned to the Welsh Highland Railway in Porthmadog. The store housed small exhibits for a while. (J.J.Davis)

11. In the same area in 1958 was the curious 1ft 10ins gauge Guinness Brewery locomotive, built by Spence in 1895. One of seven other similar machines is at the Amberley Museum in West Sussex, along with the hoist which lifted it into a haulage truck for working on 5ft 3ins track in Dublin. A wooden slate truck is on the right. (A.G.W.Garraway)

12. Standing on the rebuilt bridge on 14th June 1958 is no. 1 *Talyllyn* after a major rebuild in the Midlands. It had been out of action since about 1945 with a seriously decayed boiler, the repair of which was beyond the means of the infant TRPS in 1951. (Ll.Bedder)

13. In the background of this 1960 view is the new museum building (right) and empty BR coal wagons. The wharf was used at this time for coal and rails. Sleepers arrived by road and were cut in half for re-use and stacked as seen. (J.J.Davis)

14. Standing outside the museum in August 1961 is the metre-gauge ex-Waltham Ironstone Co. *Cambrai.* It had been built by Corpet & Cie in 1888 for the Chemin de Fer du Cambresis, in France. The locomotive departed for Oxfordshire on the 20th February 1976. (J.J.Davis)

15. By the Easter of 1967, the station extension and canopies were nearly complete and building materials were still in evidence. Nos 1 and 4 wait to depart, the Abergynolwyn refreshment van being at the front of the train. (D.J.Mitchell)

16. One of the most novel exhibits to come to the museum was *Dot*, an 18inch gauge 0-4-0 built by Beyer Peacock in 1887 for use in their works. Of similar dimensions, the former Crewe Works *Pet* has been on show here intermittently. (J.J.Davis)

17. Included in this view is a County Donegal Railway signal, a Festiniog Railway dandy car, in which horses once rode on the downhill journey, and Penrhyn Railway *George Henry*, in the background. (J.J.Davis)

18. A man sits on the TR hedge cutter and watches the passing of BR steam in the form of a filthy and numberless 4-6-0 in 1964. No wonder that the smart TR locomotives were of such appeal. Steam on the Cambrian Coast ended on 18th January 1965. (D.J.Mitchell)

19. Features of interest in November 1958, apart from the fresh rails which were from Wood Pit in Lancashire, include the 1968 museum extension, the coal elevator and, at last, the welcome provision of a water tank at the terminus. (D.J.Mitchell)

20. No. 1 of the Irish Turf Board fleet is seen as delivered in 1969 and still fitted for peat burning. It was not acquired as an exhibit, but for reconstruction from 3ft gauge to 2ft 3ins and redesign from 0-4-0WT to 0-4-2T. It had been completed by Barclays in 1948, but little used; its evolution is shown in pictures 58, 59 and 28 in that order. (D.J.Mitchell)

21. The last Winter of passenger operation here had been in 1944-45. There was adequate accommodation for all the stock at that time, but the new open coaches of the 1960s had to remain exposed to the elements during the Winter of 1968-69. (D.J.Mitchell)

No 1

RAILWAY SHOP
REFRESHMENTS
BOOKING OFFICE
WAY OUT

22. Occasional special trains have brought welcome additional revenue but also accommodation problems. No. D348 is hauling members of the Railway Correspondence & Travel Society and the TRPS on 3rd May 1969. The train had started from Leeds at 08.56. The InterCity's Landcruise trains made a number of visits in the 1980s. (D.J.Mitchell)

23. The abandonment of the Channel Tunnel project after it had started in the mid-1970s was beneficial to the TR, as a large amount of track became available. Intended for construction trains, it was of 3ft gauge; hence the spike extracting tool, seen on 5th October 1975. (D.J.Mitchell)

24. Thirty years of the TRPS was celebrated in May 1981. Carrying a DIAMOND JUBILEE headboard is no. 4 *Edward Thomas*, which was sixty years old that year and was named after the TR's manager to 1950. He did so much to secure the line's future and had worked on it since 1897.This was the first time that the TR had ever seen five locomotives in steam. A record all six were steamed on 25th September 1999. (D.J.Mitchell)

TYWYN WHARF

25. Still having occasional use in the 1990s were two ex-Corris Railway wagons which arrived with nine others and the two locomotives in March 1951. By then owned by BR, they were purchased for £1 the pair. They were photographed on the wharf in 1980. (D.J.Mitchell)

26. A panorama from 24th March 1996 features no. 3 *Sir Haydn* with a full length train of modern or reconstructed coaches. Also evident is the spacious cafe adjacent to the museum and the wharf siding curving to the left of the coal staithe. Houses have appeared in the background. (D.J.Mitchell)

27. The curved siding from the station gives access to the permanent way yard. The line on the right descends to a ballast loading dock at which tipper lorries discharge. The down platform of the main line station is in the distance. (V.Mitchell)

L & N W R

28. An impressive line up took place on 30th September 1995. From left to right are 0-4-0WT no. 6 *Douglas*, 0-4-2T no. 1 *Talyllyn*, 0-4-2T no. 3 *Sir Haydn* and 0-4-2T no. 7 *Tom Rolt*. Nos 6 and 3 are displaying their steam operated air pumps. (T.Eyres)

Pheasantry
Presbyterian Ch
(English)
Morfa-bâch
Capel Bethesda
(Ind.)
Police Station
HIGH STREET
Tyddyn-du
Well
Capel Ebenezer
(Wes. Meth)
Baptist Chapel
L.B
W.M
S.P
ATHELSTAN RD.
STATION ROAD
Intermediate School
S.B
Bryn-dedwydd
Isandula Terrace
S.P.
King's
Station
S.P

This edition was published in 1901 and the scale is about 25ins to 1 mile. The TR track layout remained unaltered until 1952. Only a limited amount of development took place in the town in that period. The Cambrian Railway is shown diagonally on the left page, Wharf station is named King's and Pendre is on the right.

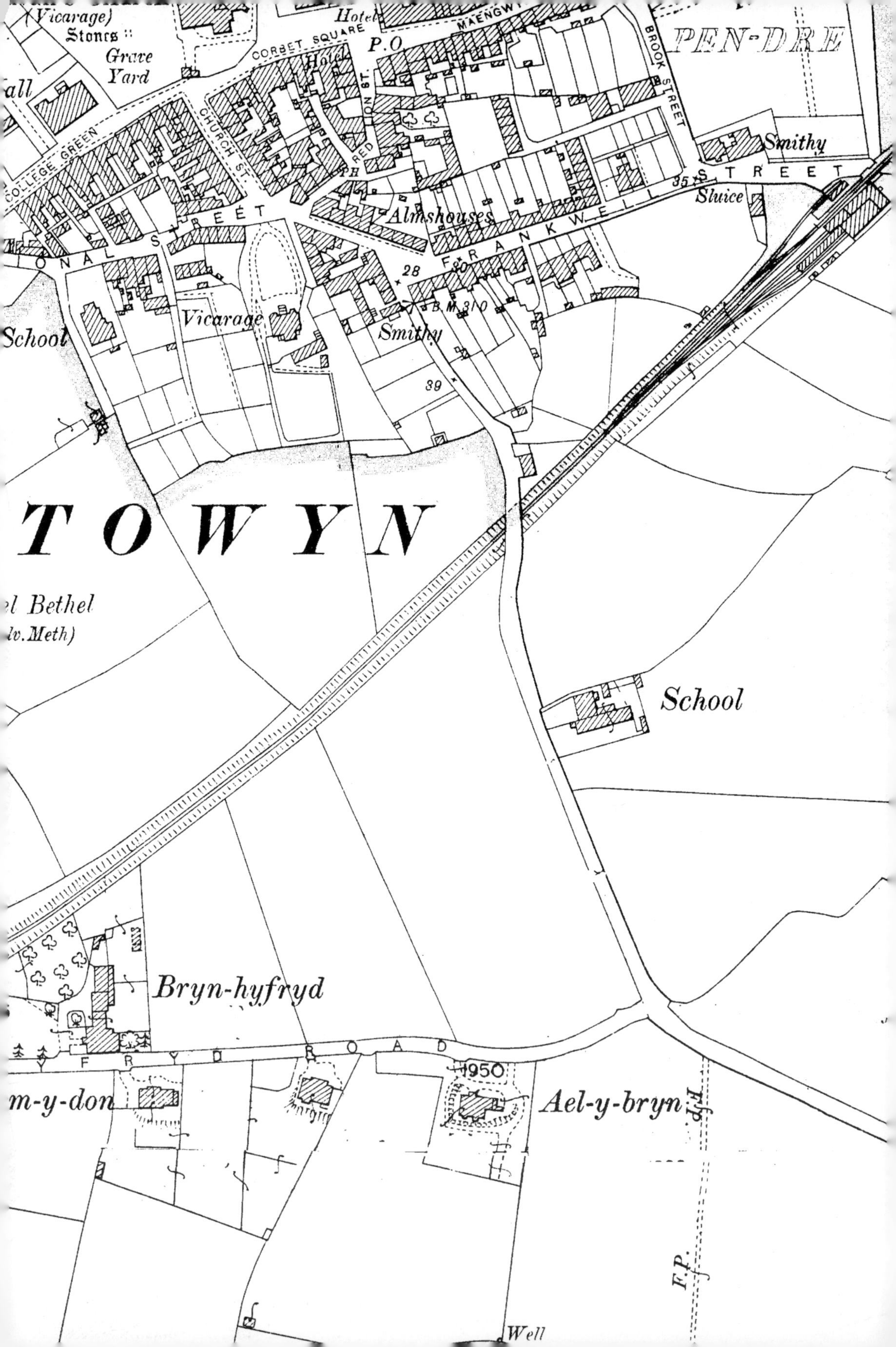
(Vicarage)
Stones
Grave Yard
Hotel
CORBET SQUARE
MAENGWY
P.O
Hotel
BROOK STREET
PEN-DRE
COLLEGE GREEN
CHURCH ST.
RED LION ST.
P.H
Smithy
STREET
35
Sluice
Almshouses
FRANKWELL
28
30
B.M. 31.0
Vicarage
School
Smithy
39
TOWYN
Bethel
School
Bryn-hyfryd
FRYD ROAD
1950
m-y-don
Ael-y-bryn
F.P.
F.P.
Well

TOWYN PENDRE

29. An eastward view from the Summer of 1951 emphasises the neglected state of the track; *Dolgoch* is waltzing towards the Wharf. To the right of her is the engine shed; the long structure housed the coaches and beyond it can be seen the roof of the workshop. Yard maintenance simply involved the use of a scythe. (A.G.W.Garraway)

30. The workshop was primitive in the extreme and devoid of electric light. Two photographs from July 1951 reveal the basic conditions, little having changed since the 1860s. No. 4 stands under the line shafting, which was driven by a Hornsby oil engine via belts, visible near the end wall. (A.G.W.Garraway)

31. At the other end of the building stood no. 3 and the forge hearth. Every effort was being made, amidst the inherited muddle, to prepare this unfamiliar engine for traffic to relieve the exhausted no. 2 and to have a standby engine available. The coupling was changed in 1954. (A.G.W.Garraway)

32. The first trial trip of no.3 was on the afternoon of Saturday 21st July 1951; author and TR manager Tom Rolt is on the left, side face is seasonal fireman John Snell, who for the last 30 years of the century gained fame as manager of an even narrower gauge railway on the Kent coast, and your author's father who, a few minutes later, was able to film no. 3 standing between the rails. It was soon revealed that the gauge had been maintained to "2 foot 3 and a thumb", for the benefit of no. 2, and that Corris tyres were narrower than those on TR engines. The disappointment was intense. (V.Mitchell)

→

33. Almost two years of track improvements were required before no. 3 could be used regularly. She was recorded on 9th June 1953 on her first and entirely successful trial that year. The large orifice in the back plate facilitated fire cleaning. (A.G.W.Garraway)

→

34. The economically clad carriage shed is on the left as no. 4 *Edward Thomas* approaches the platform on 2nd June 1953, suitably decorated on the occasion of the Coronation of Her Majesty Queen Elizabeth II. The wood was to aid locomotive fire lighting. The next four photographs were taken on the same day. (A.G.W.Garraway)

EIIR

35. Problems are bound to occur on special days, despite caution. The points had not been held over properly. Previously coaches had often been moved from the shed by hand, individually. (A.G.W.Garraway)

36. Standing close to the extremely economical carriage shed door is an ex-Penrhyn Quarry Railway vehicle, which had been regauged, numbered 7 and fitted with a roof. The TR coaches accommodated 18 passengers each, giving a train capacity of only 72 people. However, all tickets issued at that time were third class. (A.G.W.Garraway)

37. Another PQR quarrymens coach (no. 8) was returned to traffic in this form. Six had been acquired. Prior to 1951, surplus tourists had been placed in slate wagons, in which two boards had been fixed as seats. (A.G.W.Garraway)

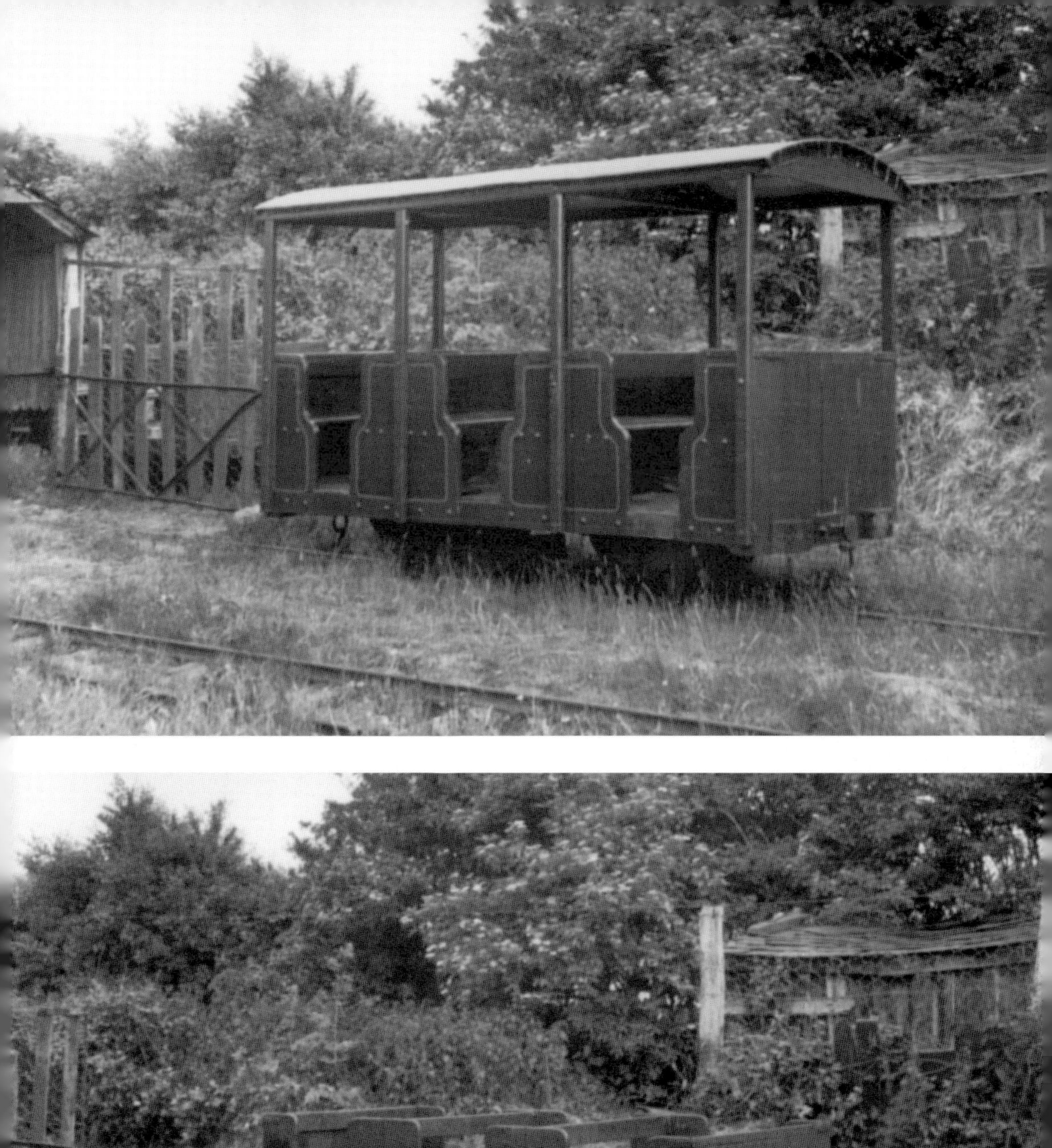

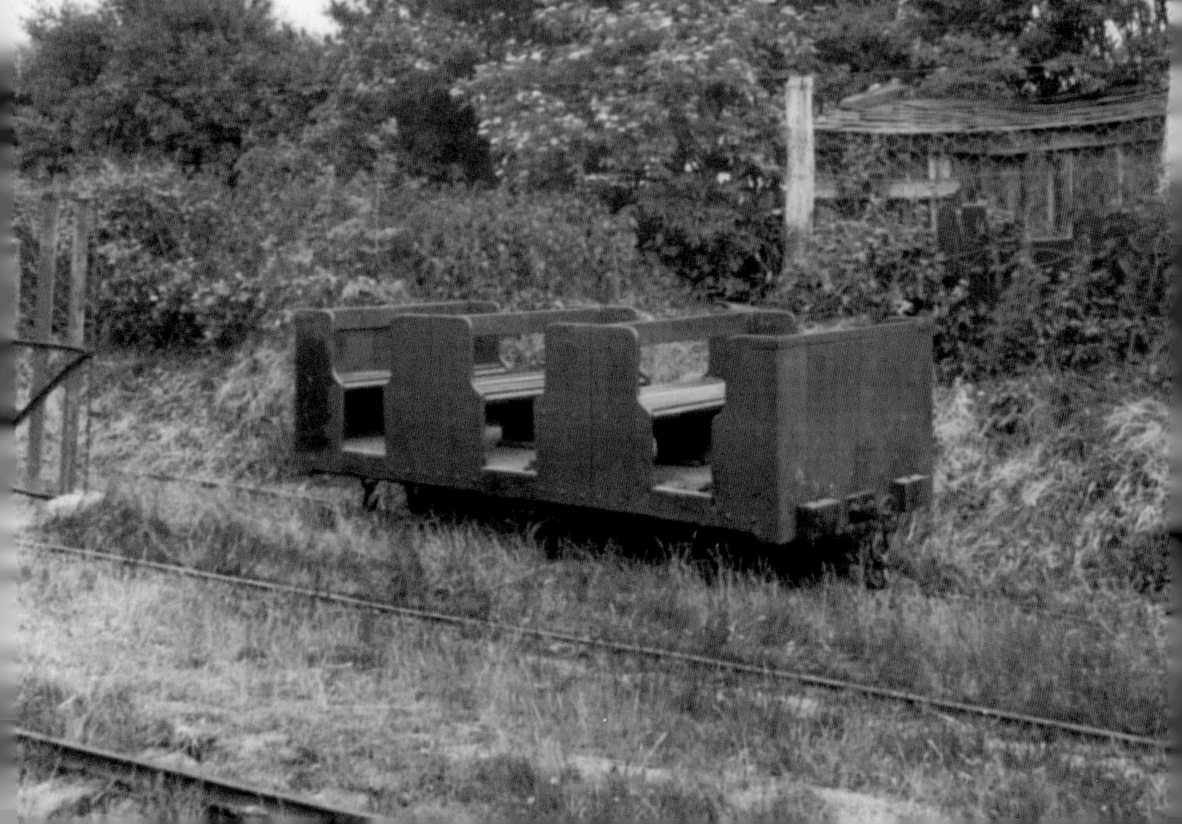

38. The final 1953 view includes the old and leaning hay store, hay harvested from the lineside having once generated income as fodder and for packing slates. Note the new water tank and that no. 3 is still facing downhill. The hay barn was near to collapse, but was used for storing no. 1 *Talyllyn* and old sleepers for firewood. (A.G.W.Garraway)

→

39. The track improvements evident in the previous picture had not reached the station by the time that this photograph was taken in 1955. Like everything else on the line, the timber-built waiting shelter and its minute booking office were life-expired. The latter had not been used for decades. (J.J.Davis)

→

40. Based on a Mercury tractor, this curious machine was slightly more successful than the one seen in picture no. 3. But, it had the disadvantage of no fast reverse gear and ran only from 1954-57. Numbered 7, it was often known as *Charlie's Ant*. (J.J.Davis)

WALES

T.R. Nº7

41. Standing on the main line on 3rd August 1957 is no. 5 *Midlander*, which was built in 1940 by Ruston & Hornsby and came to the TR in March 1957 to prove very useful. Coach no. 4 was typical of the original stock in having no door handles on the south side. (J.J.Davis)

→

42. With an expanding carriage fleet, it was necessary to destroy the hay barn in 1958 to permit the construction of the north carriage shed. This was a far-sighted act which other private railways have been slow to follow. (J.J.Davis)

→

43. Further site clearance in 1958 reduced the rural charm and gave a view of the town. Featured here are the rail carrying bolsters, the weed killing equipment and motor trolley, examples of the way in which the railway's engineering facilities were being improved. (J.J.Davis)

44. Improvements in locomotive draughting were also tried, when a Giesl ejector was fitted to no. 4, in place of its normal chimney. This special train carried Dr. Giesl on 14th September 1958. The efficiency increase was minimal and so the device was removed in 1968. (A.G.W.Garraway)

45. The new carriage shed was well advanced by the time this photograph was taken in May 1959. Also progressing was the reconstruction of ex-Corris Railway coach no. 17, which had last carried passengers in 1930. (J.J.Davis)

46. The completed and elaborately lined Corris coach was recorded providing part of the Fridays-only train for shoppers in the Winter of 1962-63. No. 5 *Midlander* is providing the power. The service was intermittent subsequently. (J.L.H.Bate)

47. No. 4's alternative to a chimney is evident as it waits to depart east. The four gates were reduced to two in 1954 by means of a welding torch, this reducing time and effort for the crossing keeper. (D.J.Mitchell)

48. Bottom discharge wagons were unusual on narrow gauge railways - these examples had once carried oil shale at Winchburgh near Edinburgh and were photographed in 1961. (J.J. Davis)

49. The workshop received several items of useful machinery, but much of it was belt driven. Right of centre, a radial drill is being moved into position. (D.J.Mitchell)

50. No. 6 *Douglas* had earlier supplied RAF flying boats on the Hampshire coast at Calshot. It has just climbed through the cutting from the Wharf in the Autumn of 1968, with ex-Corris and Glyn Valley Railway coaches behind the refreshment van. (D.J.Mitchell)

51. Reference to picture 46 will explain this situation: the engine shed windows are adjacent to *Midlander*, while those of the staff cottage are next to the coach. To accommodate more than two locomotives, the party wall was simply demolished in 1968 so that "the railroad ran through the middle of the house". (D.J.Mitchell)

52. A panorama from the water column on 31st March 1968 features both carriage sheds, together with No. 4 *Edward Thomas* near the inverted saddle tank. It is worth comparing this view with that seen in picture no. 29; progress indeed! (D.J.Mitchell)

53. A close-up of the ground frame seen left of centre in the previous picture shows that facing point locks had been fitted. The old TR avoided inspection and failed to provide many such safety devices when they became universally mandatory. (J.J.Davis)

54. As there were limited catering facilities at the inland terminus, this van was attached to the front of the first up train, as seen in picture no. 15. The attendant was liable to delay the last down train and so, to prevent this recurring, the train crew once shut up the folding counters and locked her in for the first part of the return journey. It was used from 1963 to 68. (J.J.Davis)

55. Work started on West Carriage Shed in 1970 and this is the state of progress on 17th August 1973. A signal box was included in the scheme which was not fully completed until 1984. (J.J.Davis)

REFRESHMENTS

56. No. 8 *Merseysider* arrived on the TR in 1969. It had been built by Ruston & Hornsby in 1964 for Park Gate Steel of Rotherham. It was used on their 3ft gauge system for about three years only. It had a 50hp diesel engine and hydraulic transmission. (D.J.Mitchell)

57. An operation seldom seen is the fitting of a tyre. It is first expanded by heating on a large gas ring and then the wheelset (left) is lowered into it and it is secured by contraction upon cooling. (D.J.Mitchell)

TYWYN PENDRE

58. This is our first view of the south side of the rebuilt original carriage shed and the entrance to the workshop. The boiler and firebox of the Irish locomotive, seen in picture no. 20 is about to be slid onto a new frame on 28th June 1975. Work had started in 1971, but was suspended in 1975 and resumed in 1988. (D.J.Mitchell)

59. The reconstructed locomotive is seen a little later; it became TR no. 7 and entered traffic in 1991, having been named *Tom Rolt* by his widow on 6th May of that year. Right of centre is the ex-Corris van, which had been purchased in 1951 for £2.10.0d. (D.J.Mitchell)

60. No. 9 *Alf* was built by Hunslet in 1950 for mine use and it came to the TR in 1970 to help with works trains. It was one of two obtained from Huncoat Colliery in Lancashire, the other being dismantled for spares. (D.J.Mitchell)

61. *Midlander* is standing beside the ex-Corris van and is attached to the original TR van, which doubled as a mobile booking office. Wharf was the only static location for many years at which tickets could be purchased. (D.J.Mitchell)

62. Comparison with picture 47 shows that the road had been doubled in width. This was necessary in 1984, as the farm it served had been superseded by numerous houses. No. 1 *Talyllyn* passes the new gates and the diesel oil store on 30th August 1999. (T.Eyres)

→

63. The signal box is technically PENDRE GROUND FRAME. Although it houses token instruments and functions as a block post, it has 15 levers but no signals. Flag signalling has been used since 1969, when it became possible to pass passenger trains here. The nearest part of the West Carriage Shed forms a paint shop. No. 6 heads east in 1999. (T.Eyres)

→

64. Looking in the opposite direction in 1998, we see the enlarged water tank and the original carriage shed which had been rebuilt in 1962 to serve as a supplementary engine shed. Improved toilets since 1951 meant less nutrient for nearby hedges. The portable example seen here had been in use at Dolgoch. (V.Mitchell)

MAIL
SPECIAL

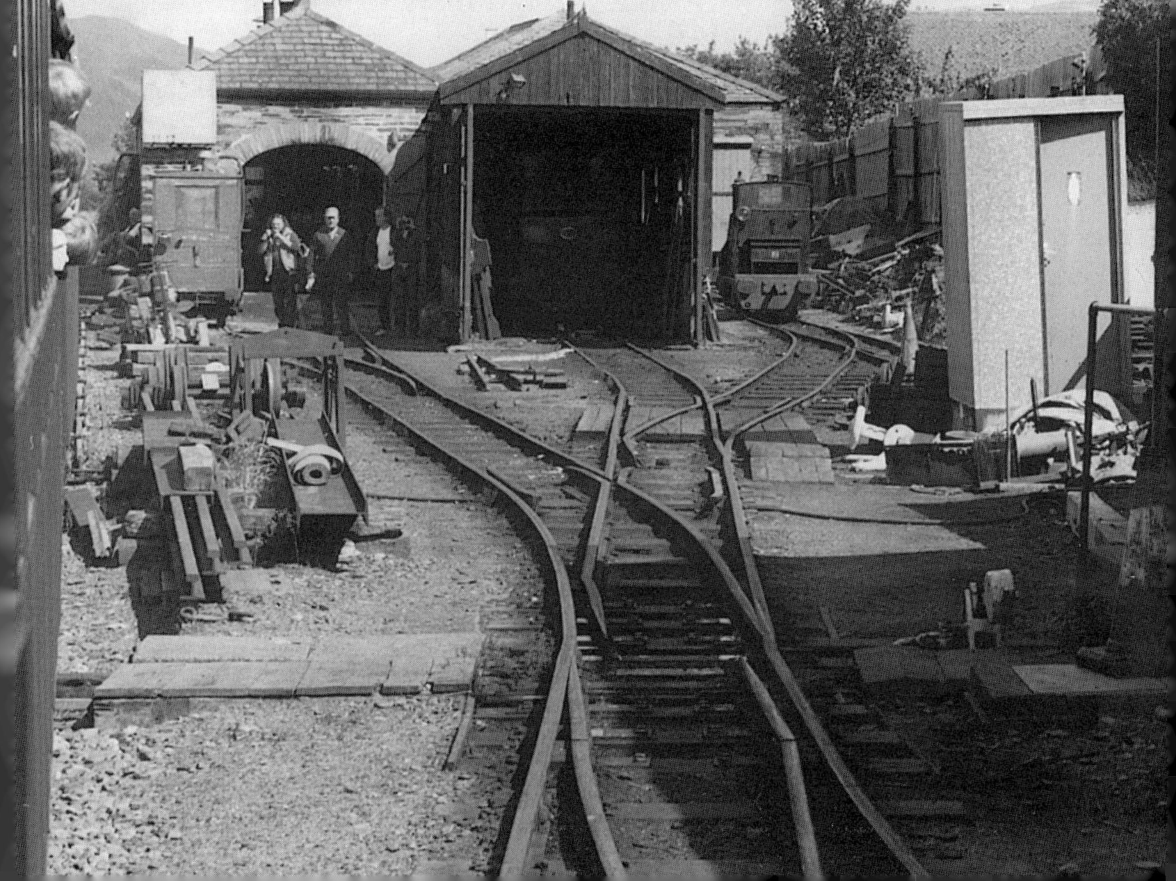

65. Hendy Farm is in the background as we admire the unchanging pastoral and arable scenery, although improvements to the electrical supply impinge upon it in this Easter 1977 view. A rail carrying train, complete with crane, descends Hendy Bank with no.3 at its head. Hendy Halt is out of view. (D.J.Mitchell)

66. No. 6 *Douglas* was out of luck on 10th August 1954, as it worked the 4.40pm from Abergynolwyn between Hendy and Ty Mawr bridges. The 5.00pm is in the background, headed by no. 4 *Edward Thomas*. (J.J.Davis)

67. Cynfal Halt (pronounced KUN-VAL) is almost two miles from Wharf and served Cynfal Farm. It is seen in 1953 after it had been exposed to view again and given a nameboard. Note that only one chair is visible; spikes and good luck sufficed elsewhere. (J.J.Davis)

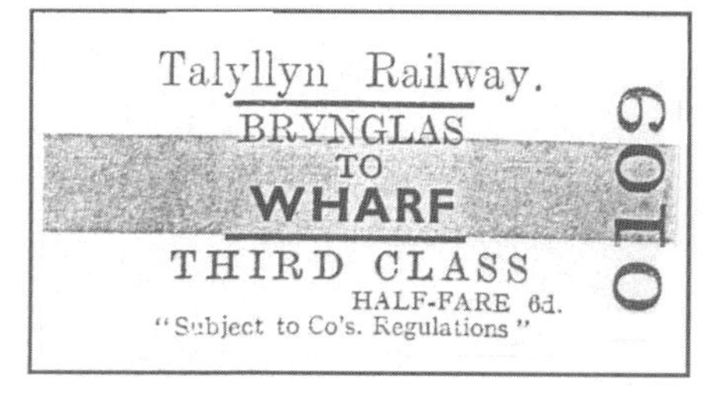

RHYDYRONEN

68. The siding was very little used, except on Whit Monday 1951, when trains terminated here and TRPS members pushed the coaches past *Dolgoch*, which stood in it at the end of each journey. A loop was laid in 1956, but removed in 1974 to permit platform lengthening. The photograph is from May 1953. (J.J.Davis)

69. The point lever is in the shadow of the leading coach as no. 3 *Sir Haydn* comes to a stand by an unusually large crowd during Easter 1969. The nearby caravan park generates some traffic. All three intermediate stations had been constructed from slate slab offcuts. (D.J.Mitchell)

70. A 1998 view reveals preservation at its best. When the station building required reroofing, slates were used. The irregular platform slabs had been reinstated for authenticity. The train is about to climb at 1 in 95, one of the steeper sections. (V.Mitchell)

BRYNGLAS

71. A bridge at the east end of the platform passes over a stream and required urgent renewal. This was undertaken on 3rd August 1952. (J.J.Davis)

The 1900 map shows a lane passing under the line west of the station, to the left of the word "Ford". It is thought that, although the bridge gave only 6ft headroom for those passing under it, its presence meant that the old TR did not have to provide gates at the crossing at the west end of the platform.

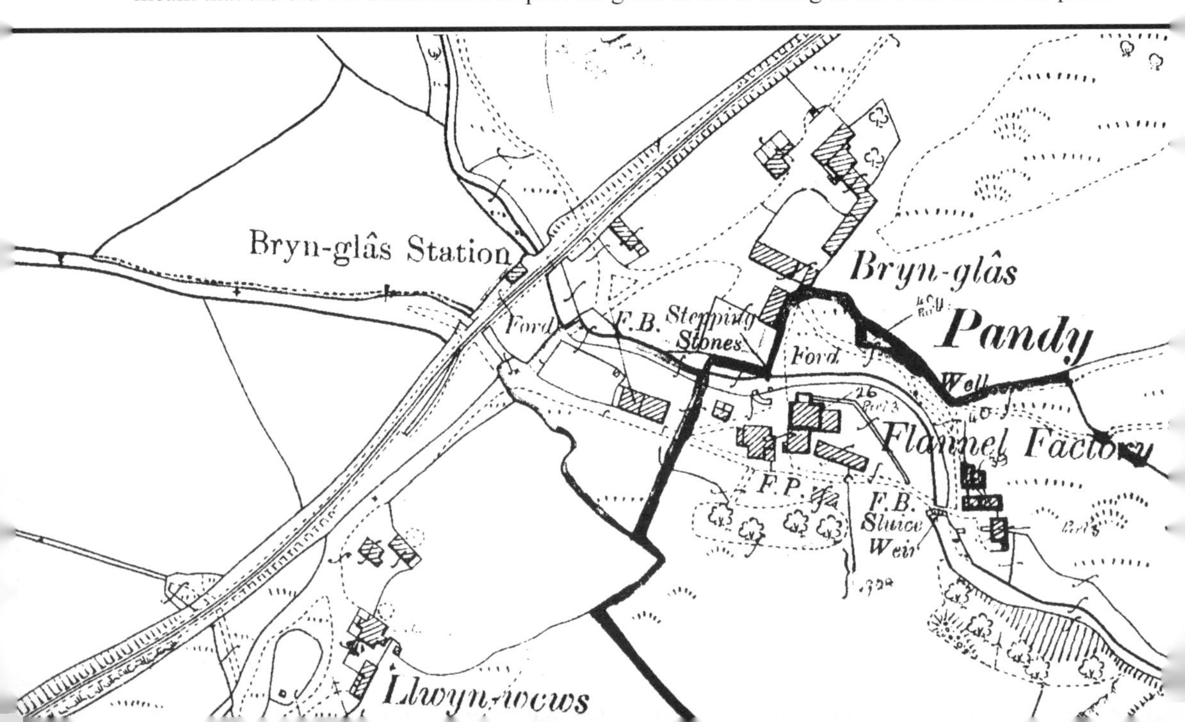

72. An eastward view from about 1955 shows that the station building is east of the level crossing on the lane that runs to the adjacent community of Pandy. No. 6 is with a works train, the rear of which carries parts of the permanent way trolley. (R.K.Walton)

73. The loop had been completed in 1953, by extending the original siding. No. 6 *Douglas* has conveyed the London Group working party in coach no. 4 and the TR van on 4th August 1956. The loop had been extended in 1954. (J.J.Davis)

74. The loop is in the background as no. 4 approaches the platform and the middle of the train passes over the level crossing on 17th August 1961. The Giesl ejector produced a unique sound that is difficult to describe. The poles gave the required clearance for the telephone wires above the road. (J.J.Davis)

75. The ground frame had been provided with a small shelter by 1969 and the telephone wires had been rerouted under the road in 1967. (J.J.Davis)

76. The loop had been extended westward in 1961 and a siding was added in 1975. No. 6 *Douglas* passes through with a freight chartered by photographers on 29th March 1998. Spot the modern road sign. (T.Eyres)

77. No. 6 passes over the bridge mentioned in caption 71, with no. 3 following, on 24th March 1972. The stream had earlier been the source of power for the woollen mill. (D.J.Mitchell)

78. When photographed in July 1972, the ground frame had a larger building to accommodate the token instruments. Electric key tokens were introduced on the sections to Pendre, and Quarry Siding in 1973, but signalling remained by coloured flag. (J.J.Davis)

DOLGOCH

79. A 1956 eastward view features the original building and platform, but the track had been relaid in 1953. Until that time, water had overflowed from the tank continuously onto the lineside. (J.J.Davis)

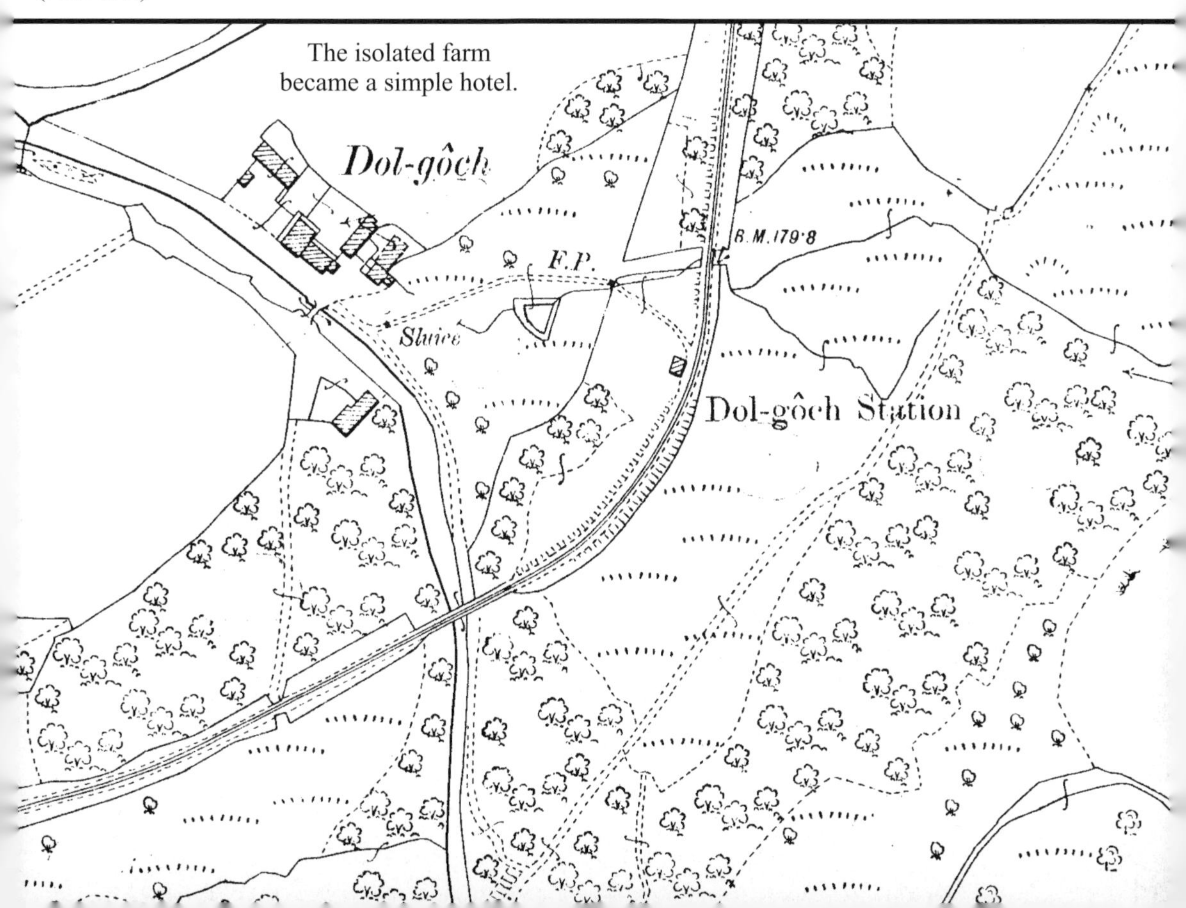

The isolated farm became a simple hotel.

80. With the advent of longer trains, a new tank was provided further east in 1961, as the platform could only be extended in that direction. No 6 stands near it - no. 3 is behind - they are on a running in turn on 24th March 1972. (D.J.Mitchell)

81. No. 2 *Dolgoch* departs from Dolgoch with an up train on 24th August 1987 on some sturdy track. Both tanks are visible. There had never been much local traffic at this location, holiday visitors being the main users of the station. A path for cattle passes under the line, below the leading coach. (D.Trevor Rowe)

82. The viaduct west of the station can now only be photographed in Winter, as tree growth has not been properly managed. No. 1 *Talyllyn* is working a private charter from Tywyn on 14th April 1996 and will soon pass under a footbridge erected for the benefit of visitors to the spectacular falls in 1957. It was opened on 9th June of that year. (T.Eyres)

EAST OF DOLGOCH

83. All the joints were originally supported in chairs and six sleepers were laid between them, only two of which bore chairs. Many of the rails had eventually been drilled and fitted with fishplates, but chaos ruled. The rails on the right had been drilled but not plated and the joint on the left has an undersize key. (J.J.Davis)

84. Your semi-exhausted author stands on the totally exhausted track on 21st June 1951, with key in hand and shovel ready to expose the next chair. Some rails had crept so that the joint was no longer over a sleeper and some chairs were not secured so that they moved along the rail, but most sleepers simply could not be seen. We took our rucksacks and tent on the trolley on this weekend of first aid mission. (V.Mitchell)

QUARRY SIDING

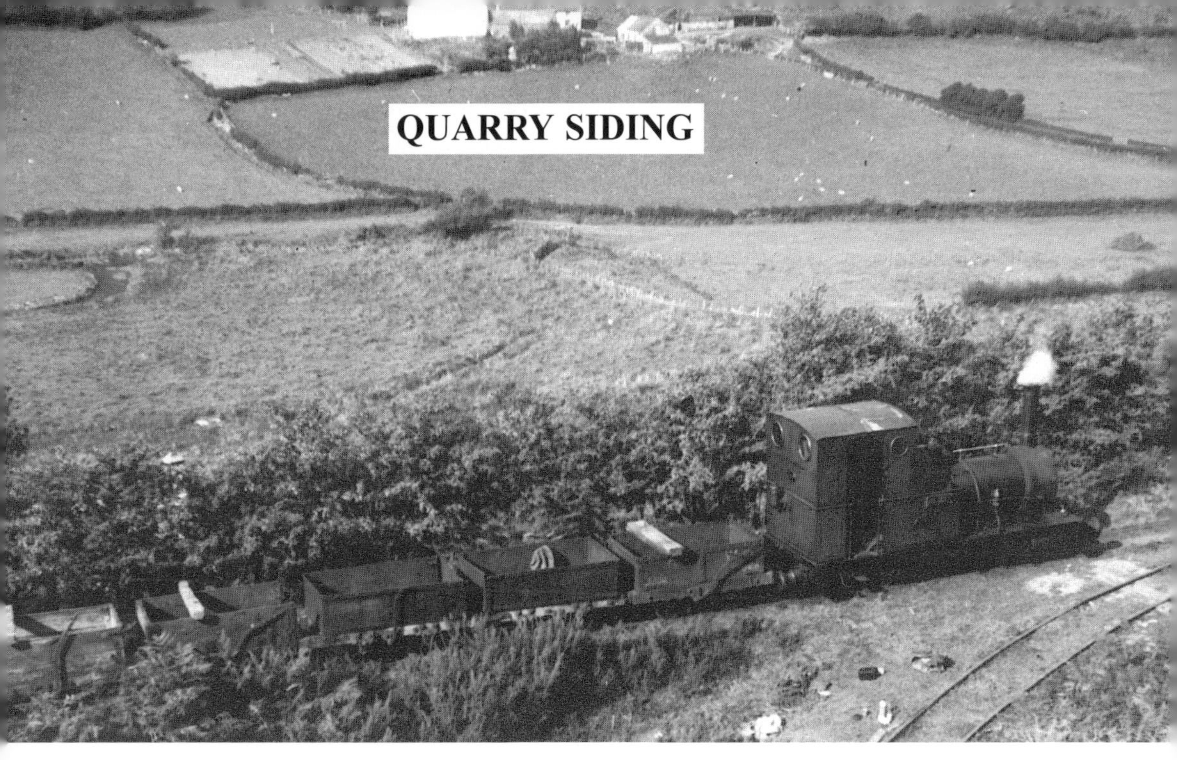

85. Less than half a mile from Dolgoch was a trailing siding on the south side, which served a disused shale quarry. It was reopened in 1952 and the material was dug for use on the track. No. 2 *Dolgoch* has arrived with a gang who travelled on the transverse timbers. (Ll.Bedder)

86. The material drained poorly and was far from ideal, but in the 1950s there was no option for financial reasons and so a loading hopper was erected. The shale also had poor lateral stability. The hopper did not work well and was seldom used. (Ll.Bedder)

87. A panorama from 1960 includes a larger radius point than the original, the siding laid in 1953, an ex-Penrhyn coach carrying the "Last Vehicle" board and the grounded body of the ex-Corris van. A replica had been built and fitted to the old chassis. (D.J.Mitchell)

88. A passing loop was laid in 1968-69 to increase line capacity; this view dates from August 1969. The quarry was little used after 1967, when the TR began to purchase used ballast from BR. (J.J.Davis)

89. A block post was established here and the ground frame cabin was photographed in 1971. The facility enabled three trains to operate simultaneously from 1969. Electric key tokens were introduced in 1973. (J.J.Davis)

90. The crew of no. 4 *Edward Thomas* wait in the loop for no. 2 *Dolgoch* to arrive on 26th May 1974. Behind the locomotive is one of the modern TR's standard coaches, built without doors on the south side. Nearest is coach no. 4 showing its unused door hinges. (D.J.Mitchell)

Talyllyn Railway
DOLGOCH
TO
ABERGYNOLWYN
THIRD CLASS
Abergynolwyn FARE 6d
'Subject to Co's. Regulations"
0257

91. The roadway seen on the left of picture 88 was upgraded for agricultural purposes and provided with a mirror (left), as direct visibility was poor. No. 3 runs west on 3rd March 1996. The siding was realigned in 1978 to serve a rail store, right. (T.Eyres)

92. Properly fitted with catch points and a facing points lock, the siding is used for works trains. The area has changed completely in 50 years. (V.Mitchell)

ABERGYNOLWYN

93. *Edward Thomas* arrives at the terminus with the third special train of the day on the occasion of the TRPS AGM on 26th September 1953. The track within sight of waiting passengers had been relaid during the previous Winter to avoid causing them alarm. The refreshments were limited to bottled drinks and confectionery. (E.D.Bruton)

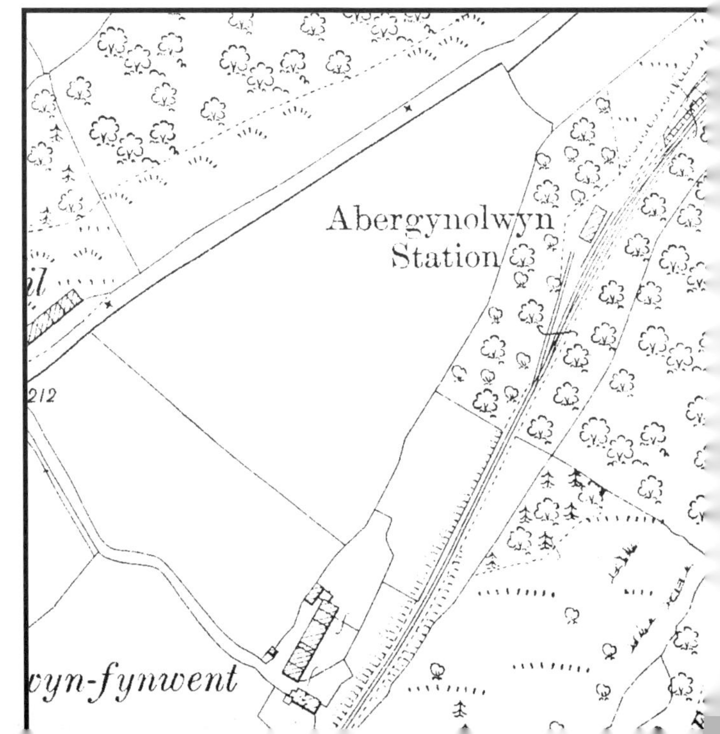

The siding was reputedly removed after World War I but was certainly in place from 1930 to 1951.

94. No. 3 ran with chimney downhill from 1953 to 1958, so that it had its only doorway on the platform side. It is seen reforming the last train of the 1954 season on 25th September. (A.G.W.Garraway)

95. A photograph from July 1965 shows the siding laid for the refreshment van, which carried the number 7 and had only one door. The building was completed in 1938 and replaced a timber structure, similar to that seen at Pendre. (J.J.Davis)

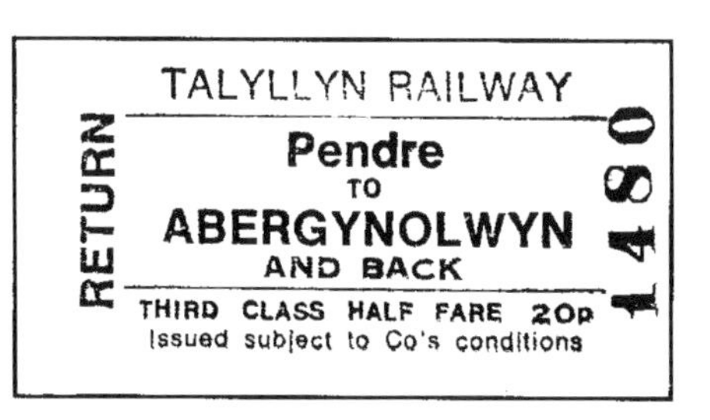

96. The site was cleared in October 1968 to make way for the third terminal building, only the sign remaining standing. The siding had been under the shrubs on the left. The hut was a temporary one for the building contractor. (A.G.W.Garraway)

97. Most of the slate blocks from the previous structure were incorporated, but wintry conditions impeded progress at times in the early months of 1969. There was no mains electricity in Abergynolwyn until 1962. (D.J.Mitchell)

98. When completed the station had electricity and a platform canopy, both firsts at this location. A small crowd awaits a down train on 11th August 1969. The Morris Minor pickup was staff transport. (J.J.Davis)

99. Further changes were to come in the 1970s, these involving the widening of the shelf on which the railway was built. Thus a tip siding was laid at the west end of the loop to dump material from the work on the extension. (D.J.Mitchell)

100. The platform line was lifted and the east points connected to another temporary tip siding. These works were preparatory to the extension of the operation to Nant Gwernol. (D.J.Mitchell)

→

101. As there was insufficient clearances on the old loop for the safe passing of passenger trains, a new loop was laid west of the building, utilising the made-up ground. The platform was lengthened onto it. (D.J.Mitchell)

→

102. The new facilities included a massive signal box, which contained only 14 levers; all signals installed were of the colour light type. The work was nearly complete by the time that this photograph of no. 2 was taken just prior to the opening of the extension in May 1976. (D.J.Mitchell)

103. Two views from August 1998 show the operating procedure. A down train waits at the west end of the long platform, while an up service passes it. The signal box is visible between the trains. Compare the tree growth with picture no. 101. (V.Mitchell)

104. Now we watch the up train gaining the platform face at the rear of the down train, which will depart once the key token has been received by the signalman - sorry, blockman. The canopy was extended outwards - compare this 1998 view of no. 7 *Tom Rolt* arriving with picture 100. (V.Mitchell)

EAST OF ABERGYNOLWYN

105. A July 1951 photograph shows the means of supplying water to locomotives at Ty Dwr, a quarter of a mile from the then terminus. Another wooden trough ducted the permanently flowing water into the engine, but the facility was seldom used after that time. This was usually when the Dolgoch supply had failed. (A.G.W.Garraway)

106. A further quarter mile along the mineral extension was the winding house for the village incline, which descended on the right. A loop line passed to the left of the building, behind which was a wagon turntable. Collapse of the timber lintel seems imminent. (D.J.Mitchell)

107. In the foreground is one of the two rails, which formed part of the crossing over the running line. The points at the top of the double track incline are shown in the background. Goods downward had included flour from Pandy Mills at Bryngl as, coal and beer. All traffic had ceased on the TR between March 1945 and Easter 1946, thus goods for the village had to go by road. However, the final few barrels of beer were lowered during the last months of 1946. (D.J.Mitchell)

Most of the lines in the village could still be seen in 1950, these having been worked by a horse from a secure compound at the foot of the incline. The tracks gave direct access to the coal sheds at the rear of most dwellings; these were owned by Haydn Jones who had provided free electricity from 1923, but it was limited to 80 watts per house! A water powered sawmill (which included the dynamo) and a writing slate factory provided some local employment. The 1886 surveyor seems to have failed to include all the wagon turntables.

108. It was possible to photograph the winding drum after the roof was removed in 1968. The brake mechanism is on the right. The main commodity upward had been "nightsoil", which was conveyed to Brynglas, where it was distributed on the fields. (D.J.Mitchell)

109. The building was demolished in 1968 for three reasons: it was becoming unsafe, it impeded the construction of the TR passenger extension and reuse of the slate blocks could save expense on the new station at Abergynolwyn. There were many members against the plan. (D.J.Mitchell)

110. The newly aligned track was also raised, using rubble from the extension. No. 2 *Dolgoch* is passing the abandoned drum soon after the new line opened in 1976. The housing for the turntable is in the foreground. Maybe, in the future, the drum could be placed in a replica winding house nearby. (D.J.Mitchell)

111. The rails from the lower quarry incline were recovered by TRPS members in 1952, using the first no. 5, seen more clearly in picture no. 3. Also visible are rails from the foot of the incline, bent vertically and of little value elsewhere. (Ll.Bedder)

112. The headland at the approach to the station had to be cut back to reduce track curvature. Much of the material was taken to the sites seen in pictures 99-101, having been loaded by this Ruston Bucyrus 10RB and hauled by no. 5.
(D.J.Mitchell)

NANT GWERNOL

113. By early 1976, the new terminal site was ready for the permanent way, but sadly much of the deep ravine was obscured from view. Van no. 7 served as a mess room; earlier it had been used for serving refreshments at Abergynolwyn, as seen in picture 95. (D.J.Mitchell)

114. A replica of Abergynolwyn's first station was built, the timber construction being advantageous in this situation, as it offered a low load on the embankment. As is usual, there was a rush to meet the opening deadline. (D.J.Mitchell)

115. Adorned with suitable regalia, no. 2 *Dolgoch* departs on opening day, 22nd May 1976, while rails remain in place on the original alignment. The last slate had passed this way in March 1948, stock from the quarry that had been closed in 1946. (D.J.Mitchell)

116. A newcomer to the area would not realise that the finely panelled coaches and the replica building were not as old as the locomotive, which is no 2. There certainly was occasion for celebration in May 1976. (D.J.Mitchell)

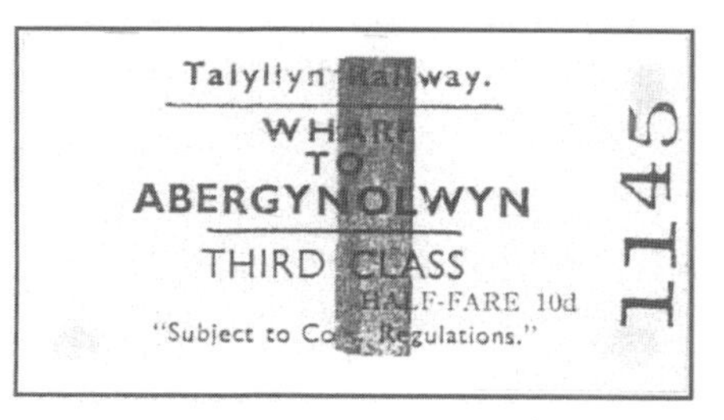
Talyllyn Railway.
WHARF
TO
ABERGYNOLWYN
THIRD CLASS
HALF-FARE 10d
"Subject to Co's. Regulations."
1145

117. No. 4 is seen in April 1996 in its temporary guise as *Peter Sam*, a character in one of the Revd.Wilbert Awdry's story books and thus a crowd puller. Note that the platform has been lengthened and a siding provided. As the equipment is evident, it should be recorded that the new operators of the TR had at last applied continuous brakes to the trains. (D.J.Mitchell)

118. The headshunt had to be cut into the foot of Alltwyllt Incline. This has an average gradient of 1 in 3.5 and is now part of a series of spectacular walks through quarry areas and forest. (V.Mitchell)

FINALE

119. It is now worth looking back to perilous days when success was by no means certain. No. 3 is seen on 18th July 1951, having been pulled from the workshop ready for its eventful first journey on 21st of that month. Mr. Rolt stands by the cabside, which was devoid of access. The unusable no. 4 is being moved through the lush grass of Pendre Yard by the frail and exhausted no. 2, which Rolt believed had its original iron boiler and copper firebox.
(A.G.W.Garraway)

120. No. 2 was suffering another health crisis when photographed in an undignified posture on 3rd October 1952. She was prone to trouble with her bearings and difficulties with her "peculiar motion". Fortunately there have been enough people (just) to keep this unique railway operational for 50 years after it nearly died.
(A.G.W.Garraway)

Middleton Press

Easebourne Lane, Midhurst, W Sussex. GU29 9AZ Tel: 01730 813169 Fax: 01730 812601

If books are not available from your local transport stockist, order direct with cheque, Visa or Mastercard, post free UK.

BRANCH LINES
Branch Line to Allhallows
Branch Line to Alton
Branch Lines around Ascot
Branch Line to Ashburton
Branch Lines around Bodmin
Branch Line to Bude
Branch Lines around Canterbury
Branch Lines around Chard & Yeovil
Branch Line to Cheddar
Branch Lines around Cromer
Branch Lines to Effingham Junction
Branch Lines around Exmouth
Branch Line to Fairford
Branch Lines around Gosport
Branch Line to Hawkhurst
Branch Line to Hayling
Branch Lines to Horsham
Branch Lines around Huntingdon
Branch Line to Kingswear
Branch Lines to Launceston & Princetown
Branch Lines to Longmoor
Branch Line to Looe
Branch Line to Lyme Regis
Branch Lines around March
Branch Lines around Midhurst
Branch Line to Minehead
Branch Line to Moretonhampstead
Branch Lines to Newport (IOW)
Branch Line to Padstow
Branch Lines around Plymouth
Branch Lines to Seaton and Sidmouth
Branch Line to Selsey
Branch Lines around Sheerness
Branch Line to Shrewsbury
Branch Line to Swanage *updated*
Branch Line to Tenterden
Branch Lines to Torrington
Branch Lines to Tunbridge Wells
Branch Line to Upwell
Branch Lines around Weymouth
Branch Lines around Wimborne
Branch Lines around Wisbech

NARROW GAUGE BRANCH LINES
Branch Line to Lynton
Branch Lines around Portmadoc 1923-46
Branch Lines around Porthmadog 1954-94
Two-Foot Gauge Survivors
Romneyrail

SOUTH COAST RAILWAYS
Ashford to Dover
Bournemouth to Weymouth
Brighton to Eastbourne
Chichester to Portsmouth
Dover to Ramsgate
Eastbourne to Hastings
Hastings to Ashford
Portsmouth to Southampton
Southampton to Bournemouth
Worthing to Chichester

SOUTHERN MAIN LINES
Basingstoke to Salisbury
Bromley South to Rochester
Charing Cross to Orpington
Crawley to Littlehampton
Dartford to Sittingbourne
East Croydon to Three Bridges
Epsom to Horsham
Exeter to Barnstaple
Exeter to Tavistock
Faversham to Dover
London Bridge to East Croydon
Orpington to Tonbridge
Tonbridge to Hastings
Salisbury to Yeovil
Swanley to Ashford
Tavistock to Plymouth
Victoria to East Croydon
Waterloo to Windsor
Waterloo to Woking
Woking to Portsmouth
Woking to Southampton
Yeovil to Exeter

EASTERN MAIN LINES
Fenchurch Street to Barking
Liverpool Street to Ilford

WESTERN MAIN LINES
Paddington to Ealing

COUNTRY RAILWAY ROUTES
Andover to Southampton
Bath to Bristol
Bath to Evercreech Junction
Bournemouth to Evercreech Jn.
Burnham to Evercreech Junction
Croydon to East Grinstead
Didcot to Winchester
East Kent Light Railway
Fareham to Salisbury
Frome to Bristol
Guildford to Redhill
Porthmadog to Blaenau
Reading to Basingstoke
Reading to Guildford
Redhill to Ashford
Salisbury to Westbury
Stratford upon Avon to Cheltenham
Strood to Paddock Wood
Taunton to Barnstaple
Wenford Bridge to Fowey
Westbury to Bath
Woking to Alton
Yeovil to Dorchester

GREAT RAILWAY ERAS
Ashford from Steam to Eurostar
Clapham Junction 50 years of change
Festiniog in the Fifties
Festiniog in the Sixties
Isle of Wight Lines 50 years of change
Railways to Victory 1944-46
SECR Centenary album
Talyllyn 50 years of change

LONDON SUBURBAN RAILWAYS
Caterham and Tattenham Corner
Charing Cross to Dartford
Clapham Jn. to Beckenham Jn.
East London Line
Finsbury Park to Alexandra Palace
Kingston and Hounslow Loops
Lewisham to Dartford
Lines around Wimbledon
London Bridge to Addiscombe
Mitcham Junction Lines
North London Line
South London Line
West Croydon to Epsom
West London Line
Willesden Junction to Richmond
Wimbledon to Epsom

STEAMING THROUGH
Steaming through Cornwall
Steaming through Kent
Steaming through West Hants
Steaming through West Sussex

TRAMWAY CLASSICS
Aldgate & Stepney Tramways
Barnet & Finchley Tramways
Bath Tramways
Bournemouth & Poole Tramways
Brighton's Tramways
Camberwell & W.Norwood Tramways
Clapham & Streatham Tramways
Dover's Tramways
East Ham & West Ham Tramways
Edgware and Willesden Tramways
Eltham & Woolwich Tramways
Embankment & Waterloo Tramways
Enfield & Wood Green Tramways
Exeter & Taunton Tramways
Gosport & Horndean Tramways
Greenwich & Dartford Tramways
Hammersmith & Hounslow Tramways
Hampstead & Highgate Tramways
Hastings Tramways
Holborn & Finsbury Tramways
Ilford & Barking Tramways
Kingston & Wimbledon Tramways
Lewisham & Catford Tramways
Liverpool Tramways 1. Eastern Routes
Liverpool Tramways 2. Southern Routes
Maidstone & Chatham Tramways
North Kent Tramways
Portsmouth's Tramways
Reading Tramways
Seaton & Eastbourne Tramways
Shepherds Bush & Uxbridge Tramway
Southampton Tramways
Southend-on-sea Tramways
Southwark & Deptford Tramways
Stamford Hill Tramways
Thanet's Tramways
Twickenham & Kingston Tramways
Victoria & Lambeth Tramways
Waltham Cross & Edmonton Tramway
Walthamstow & Leyton Tramways
Wandsworth & Battersea Tramways

TROLLEYBUS CLASSICS
Croydon Trolleybuses
Bournemouth Trolleybuses
Hastings Trolleybuses
Maidstone Trolleybuses
Reading Trolleybuses
Woolwich & Dartford Trolleybuses

WATERWAY ALBUMS
Kent and East Sussex Waterways
London to Portsmouth Waterway
Surrey Waterways
West Sussex Waterways

MILITARY BOOKS and VIDE
Battle over Portsmouth
Battle over Sussex 1940
Blitz over Sussex 1941-42
Bombers over Sussex 1943-45
Bognor at War
Military Defence of West Sussex
Secret Sussex Resistance
Sussex Home Guard
War on the Line
War on the Line VIDEO

OTHER BOOKS
Betwixt Petersfield & Midhurst
Changing Midhurst
East Grinstead Then & Now
Garraway Father & Son
Index to all Stations
South Eastern & Chatham Railways
London Chatham & Dover Railway